NEURAL NETWORKS

Easy Guide To Artificial Neural Networks

Author

Rudolph Russell

Table of Contents

Chapter 1

Introduction to Neural Networks

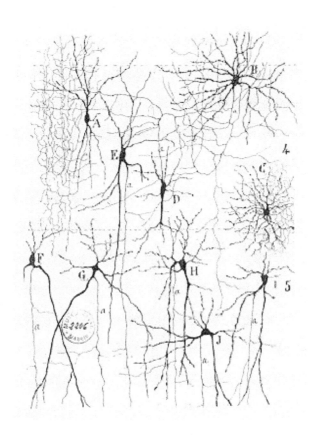

Why learn about neural networks?

In this section, we will discuss the development of artificial neural networks (ANNs), which were based on the functioning of the human brain.

Over the years, many researchers carried out experiments so that they could understand human intelligence. This research is now very useful in computing. In this chapter, we will explain how scientists use biological neural networks to create artificial neural networks. We will look at those biological neural networks that are the bases of artificial neural networks

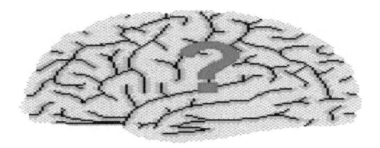

As you know, it's very easy to use neural networks in computing. They were developed with reference to a complex model of the human nervous system. You can consider them as simplified models of our brain functions.

From Neurological Research to Artificial Neural Networks

Scientists have always been fascinated by the complexity of the human brain. After many years of extensive research, we're finally able to witness the progress of this research. Before the modern era, we simply could not understand how the human brain functions. The first ANNs were developed in the 1990s.

At this time, less information about brain functions, such as perception and the way intelligence works, was available. Research focusing on specific diseases and injuries has led us to understand how our brains control movement. Our knowledge of these specific tasks, as performed by the parts of our brains, was very limited.

Research helps us understand of how these brain components help us control movement and other essential functions. We now know which parts of our brains are associated with specific kinds of injuries.

We conceived of the individual hemispheres as being well-defined, specialized systems. You can see this in the following figure, which explains the localization of various brain functions.

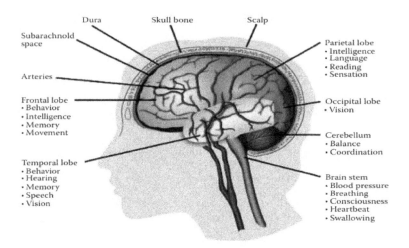

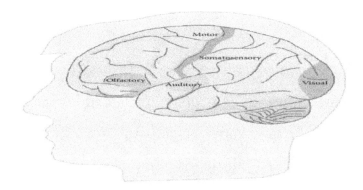

Also, in the following figure, you can understand the functions of each side of the brain.

Logic
brain

Artistic
brain

Functions of the Human Brain

However, there is also the issue of the changing of electrodes within real-life data collection. Although animal experimentation is possible, killing an animal in the name of science is rather controversial, even if it's done for a noble purpose.

It's also impossible to draw an exact conclusion regarding the human brain based on the results of animal testing. There are differences between human and animal brains, especially within the musculoskeletal and circulatory systems.

Let's take a look at the different methods that the creators of neural networks have used to work with the most desirable features and properties on the brain, as they've developed via evolution. Our brains consist of neurons that work as separate processing cells.

One neuroscientist described the human brain as a network of connected elements. They generate and send control signals to every part of the body. Indeed you'll learn more about the structures of biological neurons and their artificial equivalents, which are the core components of the structure of a neural network.

Observe, in the following figure, how an individual neuron is isolated from the web of neurons that constitutes the cerebral cortex.

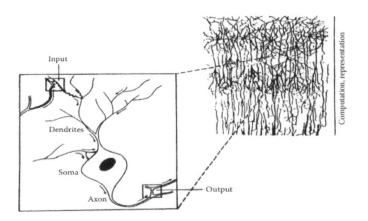

We will discuss the elements shown in the above figure in details later.

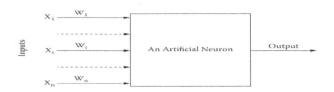

As you can see, neural neurons have an intricate and diverse construction. Artificial neural networks have trimmed down this structure. and they're also simpler in certain areas, such as the area of activity. Even though here are many differences, you can use artificial neural networks to duplicate complex behaviors.

As you can see in the last figure, the neuron can be reproduced graphically so that we can see a real neural cell. which could belong to the brain of a rat or a human, since they're quite similar. Modeling a simple ANN with a simple electronic system is very doable.

It's very easy to model both functions as one computer algorithm that show us their activities. The first neural network was built as an electronic machine, known as a perceptron.

Let's talk about how biological information is used in the field of neurocybernetics to develop neural networks. The scientists that created the first neural networks understood the actions of the natural neurons. The most important thing they discovered c was about the process by which one neuron passes a signal to another neuron.

The scientists noted that, while processing information, those large and complicated cells that take care of communication between the neurons are the most important. The synapses are also important participants in the process. They're very small, so optical microscopes are required to see them.

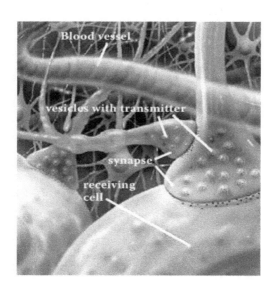

A British neuroscientist proved that, while the neural signal goes through the synapse, chemical substances called neuromodulators are engaged. They are always released at the final point of the axon, from the neurons that transfer the information, which is then sent to the postsynaptic membrane of the receiver (another neuron).

Teaching any neuron always depends on the strength of a signal that is sent by an axon from a transmitting cell, so that a very large or very small quantity of the mediator is sent to the synapse that will receive that signal.

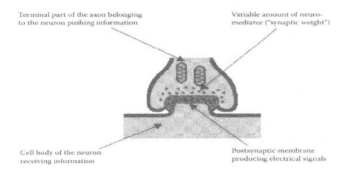

Terminal part of the axon belonging to the neuron pushing information

Variable amount of neuro-mediator ("synaptic weight")

Cell body of the neuron receiving information

Postsynaptic membrane producing electrical signals

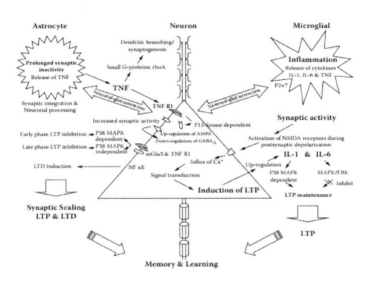

Astrocyte

Neuron

Microglial

Dendritic branching/ synaptogenesis

Prolonged synaptic inactivity
Release of TNF

Small G-proteins: rhoA

Inflammation
Release of cytokines
IL-1, IL-6 & TNF

TNF

TNF R1

P2×7

Synaptic integration & Neuronal processing

Neuronal-glial interaction

Neuronal-glial interaction

Increased synaptic activity

Synaptic activity

Early phase LTP inhibition ← P38 MAPK dependent

P13-kinase dependent

Up-regulation of AMPA

Activation of NMDA receptors during postsynaptic depolarization

Late phase LTP inhibition ← P38 MAPK independent

Down-regulation of GABA$_A$

mGlu5 & TNF R1

IL-1 & IL-6

LTD Induction

NF κB

Influx of Ca$^+$

Signal transduction

Up-regulation

P38 MAPK dependent

MAPK/ERK

Inhibit

Induction of LTP

LTP maintenance

Synaptic Scaling
LTP & LTD

LTP

Memory & Learning

Questions

1. Describe the biological structure of a neuron?.

2. What is the main function of a neuron.

3. List the functions of each side of the brain.

4. What are the functions of temporal lobe.

Chapter 2

Structures of Neural Networks

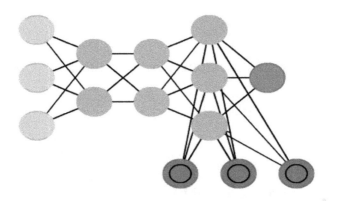

Building a Neural Network

When we were young, we tried to understand how the world
functions: for example by breaking an alarm clock into
pieces, or opening up a tape recorder to see what lies inside.
In that vein, let us try give a simple explanation of how a
neural network is built. As we explained in the previous
section, a neural network is a system that performs
calculations, based on the activities of elements called
neurons.

Artificial neural networks are always based on many lot of neurons. On the other hand, biological neurons are connected in a less complicated way. The ANN model of something like a real nervous system will be very difficult to control.

In the following figure, you can see how an artificial neural network is based on other structure and schema of our real - life nervous systems.

You might notice that the structure isn't very clear, but nevertheless it's very complex. It's like a vast forest.

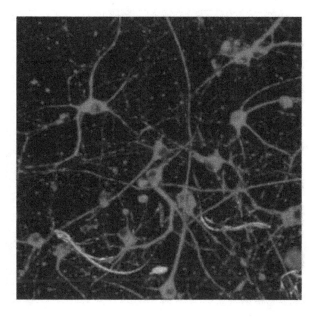

Artificial neural networks are always built so that their structures will be easy to trace, and also so that they might be used and produced very economically. In fact, these structures may be flat (one- or two-dimensional), and regularly repeated, with layers of artificial neurons. They have a well-defined objective, and are linked according to a very simple structure. As you can see in the following figure, which shows a common neural network structure, an ANN is simple in comparison to a biological network. There are three factors that affect the properties and possibilities of an artificial neural network:

1. The elements that are used to build the network (how the neurons look and work);

2. How we can connect the neurons with each other; and

3. How to establish the arguments and the parameters of your network via the learning process,

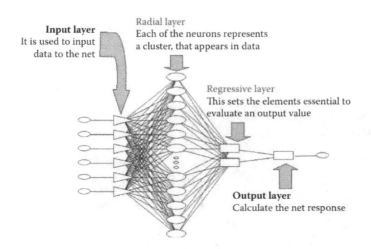

The Construction of Artificial Neurons

The basic buildings materials used to create neural network
are artificial neurons, and we should learn about them in
great detail. In the last section, we discussed biological
neurons.

In the following figure, you'll find a simple depiction of a
neuron. Not every neuron looks like this, but most do.

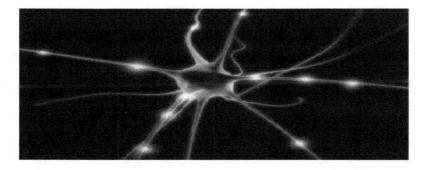

In the following figure, you can see a biological neuron that is part a rat's cerebral cortex.

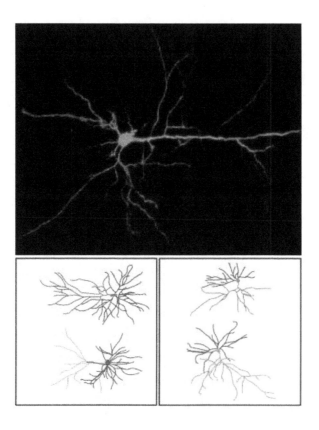

It's very difficult to observe the differences between an axon, which delivers signals from a specific neuron to all the other neurons, and a dendrite, which serves a special purpose from the maze of fibers seen in the figure. Artificial neural networks have all the features necessary for completing tasks they're characterized by many inputs, but one output only.

The signals of the input, Xi, I = 1 or 2 or 3 ...n, and the signal of the output, y, may take only one numerical value. In fact, the tasks will be solved via information that is the result or the output of a specific protocol. Generally, each input and output are associated with a specific definition for any given signal. In addition, the signal extension is used, so that the selected values of a signal within a network will not be outside of an agreed-upon protocol or range; for example, from 0 to 3, and so on.

Artificial neurons perform dedicated activities on input signals and produce output signals (just one for a single neuron). This means forwarding them to the other neurons or to the output of the network. This is called network assignment; used to reduce the functioning to its basic neural elements. This is based on the fact that it transforms an input, x, of data into an output, y, of data by applying the rules that are learned and also assigned at the time the network is created. You can see how this works in the following figure.

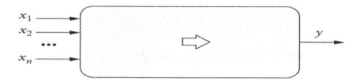

They can learn to use those coefficients that are synaptic. The neurons reflect the complex biochemical and bioelectric processes that take place in biological neural synapses. These kind of weights constitute the basis of a teaching network, which can be modified.

Adding variable weight coefficients to a neuron structure makes it a learnable unit. You can think of the ANNs as computer processors with dedicated features, as described below. Every neuron receives many input signals, Xi, and, on the basis of the inputs, determines its answer, y, with a single output signal. A weight parameter called WI is connected to separate neuron inputs. It expresses the degree of importance of information that comes to a neuron using a specific input, xi. A signal arriving via a particular input is first modified with the use of the weight of the input.

Most often, the modification is based on the fact that a signal is simply multiplied by the weight of a given input.

Consequently, in later calculations, this signal will participate in another form.

The signal is very strong if the weight value is higher than 1 or smaller than 1. This signal from a specific input will appear in the opposite signals from the inputs if the weight of the input has a value of less than 1. Inputs with negative weights are defined by neural network users as inhibitory inputs; those with positive weights are called excitatory inputs. Input signals are aggregated in a neuron.

Networks use many methods of aggregating input signals. In fact, aggregations are simply adding input signals to determine internal signals.

This is referred as cumulative neuron stimulation or postsynaptic stimulation. This signal may be also defined as a network value. Maybe a neuron adds an extra component, independent of input signals, to the created sum of signals.

We can call it a bias, and it actually goes through the learning methods. So, a bias will be considered as an extra weight associated with inputs, and it provides an internal signal of constant value equal to 1.

A bias helps in the formation of a neuron's properties during the learning phase, when the function properties don't need to pass through the beginning of the coordinate system.

The following figure depicts a neuron with a bias. The sum of internal signals multiplied by weights, in addition to a bias, may sometimes be sent directly to its axon and treated as a neuron's output signal. This works well for linear systems,

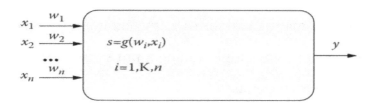

something like adaptive linear networks. In a network with more capabilities, such as a multilayer perceptron, the output of the neuron signal will be calculated via many functions. The symbol $f()$ or $\varphi()$ is used to represent the function . Below, the figure depicts a neuron, including both input signal aggregation and output signal generation. Function $\varphi()$ is a characteristic of a neuron.

Other characteristics of neurons exist as well. But some of them are chosen, so that the behavior of an artificial neuron resembles that of a biological neuron, but with characteristics that can also be selected in a manner that ensures the full efficiency of computations carried on by a neural network.

At all times, function φ () constructs an important element between a joint stimulation of a neuron and its output signal. Knowledge of the inputs, weight coefficients, input aggregation methods, and neuron characteristics, allowed to unequivocally define the output signal at any time, always assumes

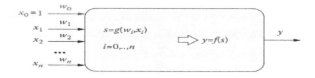

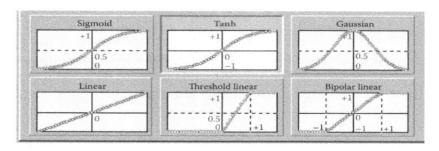

that the process appears instantly, contrary to what happens with biological neurons. This will help the ANNs reflect changes in the input signals instantly at the output. This is a clearly theoretical assumption. After input signals change, even in electronic realizations, some time is needed to establish the correct value of an output signal with an adequate integrated circuit.

More time would be necessary to achieve the same effect in a simulation: a computer imitating network activities needs to calculate all values of all signals on all outputs of all neurons in a network.

This would require a lot of time, even with very fast computers. You'll not pay attention to neuron reaction time in discussions of network functioning because it's a trivial factor in this context.

This neuron presented in this figure is the typical model that will be used to create a neural network. In fact, this neural network material is made up of neurons known as perceptrons. This neuron is referred to by the aggregation function consisting of simple summing of input signals, multiplied by weights, and uses a nonlinear transfer function with a distinctive sigmoid shape.

Radial neurons are sometimes used for special purposes. They involve an atypical method of input data aggregation, use specific properties, and are taught in an unusual manner.

We will not go into elaborate details about these specific neurons, which are used mainly to create special networks known as radial basis functions.

The Biological Neurons Model

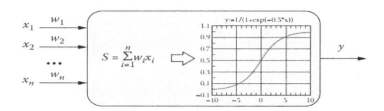

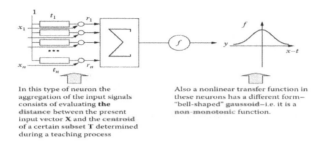

In this type of neuron the aggregation of the input signals consists of evaluating **the** distance between the present input vector **X** and the centroid of a certain subset **T** determined during a teaching process

Also a nonlinear transfer function in these neurons has a different form— "bell-shaped" gaussoid—i.e. it is a non-monotonic function.

After many years, scientist Schutter tried to model in the structure and functioning of just one neuron, the Purkinje, in detail. The model uses an electric system that, according to Hodgkin and Huxley, modeled bioelectrical activities of individual fibers and the cell membranes of neuron soma.

After considering other research on the functioning of so-called ions channels, he was successful in generating the shape of a real Purkinje cell with extraordinary accuracy. The model turned out to be very complicated and involved costly calculations.

For example, it required 1,600 so-called compartments (cell fragments treated as homogeneous parts containing specific substances in specific concentrations), 8,021 models of ions channels, more than 9 different complicated mathematical descriptions of ion channels dependent on voltage, more than 30,000 differential equations, more than 19,000 parameters to estimate the tuning of the model, and a precise description of cell morphology, based on precise microscopic images. It's no surprise that many hours of continuous work on a large supercomputer were needed to simulate several seconds of "life" of such a nerve cell.

Despite this issue, the results of the modeling were very impressive, and unambiguous. This attempt at faithfully modeling the structure and action of a real biological neuron was successful, but simply too expensive for creating practical neural networks for widespread use.

When researchers used only simplified models. Despite their, we know that neural networks can solve certain problems effectively, and they even allow us to draw interesting conclusions about the behavior of the human brain.

How They Work

The first description of ANNs indicates that each neuron possesses a specific internal memory (we can represent them by the values of current weights and bias) and certain abilities to convert input signals into output signals.

It bears noting that these abilities are rather limited. A neuron is like a cheap processor within a system that contains maybe thousands of such elements.

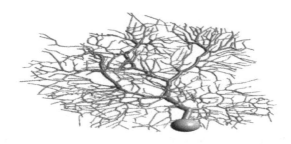

ANNs are useful components of systems that can process very complex data-based tasks. A neural network is the result of the limited amount of information gathered by a single neuron and its poor computing capabilities. It consists of several neurons that can act only as a whole.

Thus, all the capabilities and properties of neural networks mentioned earlier result from collective performances of many connected elements that constitute the whole network. This specialty of computer science is known as massive parallel processing.

Now, let's examine the operational details of a neural network. It's clear from the above discussion that the network program, the information that constitutes knowledge database, and the data can be calculated, and the calculation processes are all completely distributed.

It's not possible to point to an area where specific information is stored, even though neural networks may function as memories, especially as so-called associative memories have shown impressive performance. It's also impossible to connect certain areas of a network to a given part of the algorithm that was used : for example, to indicate which network elements are responsible for initial processing and analysis and which elements produce final network results.

We will now analyze how a neural network works and what roles the single elements play in the whole operation. You may assume that all network weights are already determined (for example, that e teaching process has been accomplished).

The important process of teaching a network is rather complex process. We begin our analysis by the from the point where a new task is presented to a network. The task can be represented by a number of input signals appearing at all inputs.

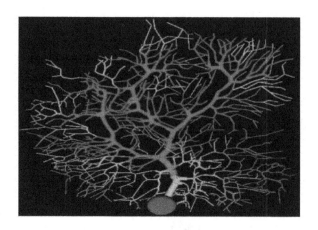

The signals may be represented by red dots. These input signals reach the neurons in the input layer. These neurons usually don't process the signals; they only distribute them to the neurons in the hidden layer. The distinct nature of the input layer neurons that only distribute signals, rather than process them, is generally represented graphically by various types of symbols (e.g., a triangle instead of a square).

The next step involves activation of the neurons in the hidden layer. The neurons use their weights (hence utilizing the data they contain), first to modify the input signals and aggregate them, and then, accordingly to their characteristics calculate the output signals that are directed to the neurons in the output layer.

This stage of data processing is crucial for neural networks. Although the layer doesn't occur externally (the signals will not be registered at the input or output ports), this is the layer where most of the task-solving activity is performed. Most of the network connections and their weights are located between the input and the hidden layers.

We can say that the most of the data in the teaching process is in this layer. These signals will be provided through the layer (hidden). Neurons don't have direct contradictions, unlike the input or the output signals—each signal will have a meaning for the task that is solved—but with this process, the layer of the neurons provide not full products.

That is, signals specify the task in such a way that it's relatively easy to use each of them.

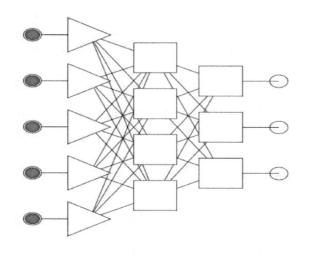

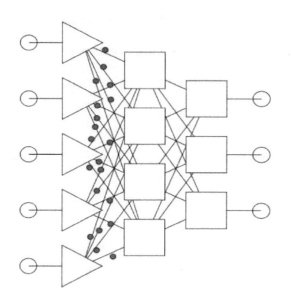

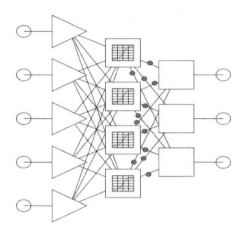

By working with the performance of the network at the last stage of solved task, you can see that the layer of neurons will take features of their abilities to sum up the signals and their properties to build the last solution at the network output ports.

In other words, a network always works as a whole, and all its elements contribute to performing all the tasks of the network. This process is similar to a holographic reproduction, in which one can reproduce a complete picture of a photographed object using the pieces of a broken photographic plate.

One of the advantages of network performance is its excellent ability to work properly, even after a significant part of its elements fail. One scientist has taken his some of his network's capabilities (like the letter recognition method) and then tested them as he damaged more and more of their elements. These networks were special electronic circuits. Though Rosenblatt would damage an important part of a network, it would continue to function properly.

The failure of a higher number of neurons and connections would cause the quality of performance to deteriorate, in that the damaged part of the network would make more mistakes (as an example, to recognizing O as D) but it would not fail working.

Compare this behavior to the fact that the failure of a single element of a modern electronic device, such as a computer or television, can cause it to stop working entirely. More than thousands of neurons within the brain die every day for many reasons, but our brains continue to work unfailingly throughout our lives.

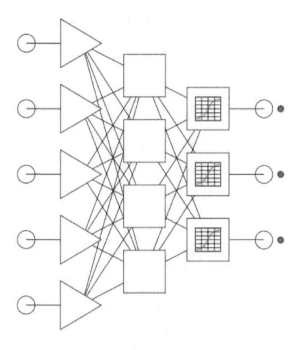

The Capabilities of Neural Network Structure

You can consider the relationship between the structure of a neural network and the tasks that it can perform. We also know that the neurons explained before are used to create neural networks.

Network structures are created by connecting outputs of certain neurons with inputs of other neurons, based on a specific design. The result is a system of parallel and max concurrent processing of diverse information. When keeping all these factors, we always choose layer-structured networks, and connections between layers are made on a one-to-one basis. Obviously, the specific topology of a network (the number of neurons in layers) should be based on the types of tasks the network will process.

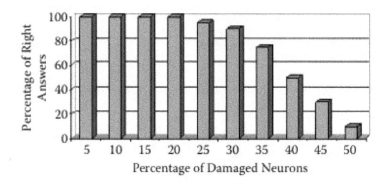

In this theory, the rule is simple: the more complex the task, the more neurons are needed to solve it. A network with more neurons is simply more intelligent. To be practical, this concept isn't as unequivocal as it appears. The concept of neural networks **contains huge works**, proving that decisions regarding the network structure affect its behavior far less than expected.

This paradoxical statement derives from the fact that behavior of a network is specified fundamentally by the network teaching process, not by its structure or the number of elements it contains.

This explains how a well-taught neural network, which has a specific structure, can solve tasks in a more efficient way than a badly trained network with a proper structure. Many experiments performed on neural network structures, created by randomly deciding which elements connect, and in what way. Despite their casual designs, the networks were capable of solving complex tasks.

Let's take a closer look at the important consequences of this random design. If a randomly designed network can achieve correct results despite its structure, its teaching process can thus allow it to adjust its parameters to operate as required, based on a chosen algorithm. This means that the system will run correctly, despite its fully randomized structure.

These experiments were first performed in the early 1970s. The scientist flipped the dice or drew straws and, based on the final results, connected specified elements of a network together. The resulting structure was completely chaotic. After teaching, the network could solve tasks effectively.

The scientist's reports of his experiments were so astonishing that other scientists did not believe his results were possible until the experiments were repeated. This system, which was similar to the perceptron built by Rosenblatt, was developed and studied around the world.

Networks that don't have a standard connection can always learn to solve tasks correctly; however, the teaching process for a random network is more complex and time-consuming when compared to the teaching of a network whose structure is reasonably related to the task at hand.

It's interesting to note that philosophers were also interested in the researchers' results. They claimed that the final results proved a theory given, and then later modified, by other scientists.

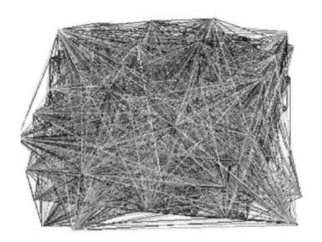

The researcher proved that this concept is technically possible, essentially, in the form of neural networks. Another problem is whether the concept works for all humans.

The other scientist claimed that early abilities amounted to nothing, and newly gained knowledge was everything. You can't comment on the researcher's statement, but we do know that neural networks gain all their knowledge only by having their learning methods adjusted to the task structure.

Of course, the network structure must be complicated enough to allow "crystallization" of the needed connections and structures. A network that is too small will never learn anything because its "intellectual potential" is inadequate.

This important issue is the number of elements involved, not the design of the structure.

For example, no one teaches relativity theory to a rat even though the rat may have been trained to find a way through complicated labyrinths. Similarly, no human is programmed at birth to be a surgeon, an architect, or a laborer. Jobs and careers are choices. No statement about equality can change the fact that some individuals have remarkable intellectual resources and some don't.

You can apply this idea to network design. You can't create neural networks using early technology; however, it's not too difficult to create a cybernetic troglodyte, which has so few neurons that it can't learn anything. A network can perform widely diverse and complex tasks if it's large enough. Although it seems that a network can't be too big, a larger size can create complications.

Studies prove that a network will solve a problem; a neural structure is naturally more valuable. A reasonably designed structure, which fits the problem' requirements at the beginning, can shorten learning time significantly, and improve results.

This is why we want to discuss the construction of neural networks, even though it may not provide the solution for all kinds of construction problems. Choosing a solution to a construction problem without sufficient information is rather difficult, if not impossible.

Constructing neural networks so that it can be adapted to any structure is similar to the problem of the inexperienced software engineer who is confused by the system message stating "press any key" . What key? You may laugh about that, but we hear a similar question from our graduate students: what is "any structure" of a neural network?

We must now note a few facts about common neural network structures. Not all aspects of all structures are completely understood. You can start by categorizing commonly used network structures to two sub-classes: neural networks with and without feedback.

Neural networks without feedback are often called feed-forward types. Networks in which signals can circulate for an unlimited amount of time are called recurrent. These signals begin going from the input and the data relevant to this problem will arrive in the neural network, to get the output in which the neural network will provide a result. These types of networks are the most frequently used.

Recurrent networks are characterized by feedback. Signals can circulate between neurons for a very long time before they reach a fixed state. In many cases, the network can't provide fixed states.

The connections presented as red (external) arrows are feedbacks, so the network depicted is recurrent. Recurrent network properties and abilities are more complex than those of feed-forward networks. Additionally, their computational potentials are astonishingly different from those of other types of neural networks. For instance, they can solve optimization problems.

They can search for the best possible solutions—a task that is almost impossible for feed-forward networks.. In Hopfield networks, the one and only type of connection between neurons is feedback. In the past, the development of the solution to the famous traveling salesman problem by a Hopfield network was a global sensation. Given a set of cities and the distance between each possible pair, the traveling salesman problem entails finding the best possible way of visiting all the cities exactly once before returning to the starting point.

A solution to this problem using neural networks was presented for the first time in a paper by Hopfield and Tank.

Questions

1. Describe the difference between biological and artificial neural networks.

2. What are the capabilities of neural network structure?

Chapter 3

Teaching Your Networks

Neural network activity can be categorized into various stages of learning, during which the network collects the information needed to determine what it will do and how, and the steps of regular work when the network should solve dedicated new tasks depending on the collected knowledge.

The most important thing to understanding how a network works and the abilities it has is the learning process. Two variations of learning can be distinguished: one that requires a teacher and one that doesn't. we're going to talk about learning without a teacher in the next chapter.

This chapter will focus on learning with a tutor. Such learning is based on giving the network examples of correct actions that it should learn to mimic. An example normally includes a specific set of input and output signals, given by a teacher, to show the expected response of the network for a given setup of input data.

The network observes the connection between input data and the required outcome and learns to imitate the rule. While learning with a tutor you always have to deal with a pair of values: a sample input signal and a desired output (required response) of the network to the input signal. Of course, a network can have many inputs and many outputs.

The *pair*, in fact, represents a complete set of input data and output data that should work as a complete solution for a task. The two components (the data for a task and the output solution) are always required. The *teacher* and *tutor* terms require explanations at this point. A tutor isn't necessarily a human being who teaches a network, even though humans work with and instruct networks.

In practice, the role of a tutor is taken over by a computer that models the specific network. Unfortunately, neural networks aren't very smart. Effective learning a difficult task requires thousands, or sometimes even hundreds of thousands, of steps! No human would have the strength and patience to tutor a device that learns so slowly.

That is why a teacher, or tutor in this context, refers to a computer program, supplied by a human, with a so-called learning set. What is a learning set? Here is a table showing sample data concerning pollution rates in various US cities. Any other type of data could be used to explain this concept. However, it is important to use real-life data.

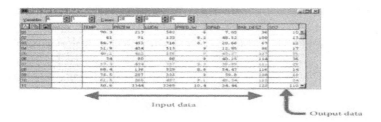

In a real database, I explained that, after leaving the elements of the original window (a program operating on this database)--the data collected in the database, as you can see-- we can isolate those that will be used as outputs for the network.

Check out the range of columns of the table with the arrow at the bottom of the figure. The data will allow us to predict many levels of air pollution. The data covers population figures, industrialization levels, weather conditions, and other factors. When these data are used as inputs, the network will have to predict the average level of air pollution in every city. For a city in which pollution level information has not been compiled, we will have to guess.

That is where a previously educated network will go to work. The learning set data—known pollution data for several cities—has been placed in an appropriate column on the table, which is marked with a red arrow (output).

Therefore, you have exactly the material you need to teach the network: a set of data pairs containing the appropriate input and output data. We can see the causes (population, industrialization, and weather conditions) and the result (air pollution value).

With this strategy, the network uses these data and will learn how to function properly (estimating the values of air pollution in cities for which proper measurements have not yet been made).

Exemplary learning strategies will be thoroughly discussed later. In the meantime, another detail of that. The letters in one column of the table are barely visible because they appear in gray instead of black.

This shading suggests that the data portrayed are somewhat less important. The column contains the names of particular cities.

Based on this information, the database generates new data and results, but, for a neural network the information in the columns is useless. The level of air pollution isn't related to the name of a city, so, even though these names are available in the database, we won't use them to teach networks.

Databases often contain a lot of information data that isn't needed to teach a network. We should remember that the tutor involved in network learning will usually be a collection of data that isn't used "as is," but is adjusted to function as a learning set following cautious selection and proper setup (data to be used as inputs and data to be generated as outputs).

A network should not be littered with data that a user knows isn't useful for checking solutions to a specific problem.

Besides the method of the learning with a teacher described earlier, a series of methods of learning without a teacher (self-learning) is also possible. The methods only consist of passing a series of test data to the input of networks, without counting desirable or even anticipated output signals.

It seems that a properly designed neural network can use only observations of entrance signals to build a sensible algorithm of its own activity based on them, most often relying on the fact that classes of repeated (maybe with certain variety) input signals are automatically detected and the network learns (spontaneously, without any open learning) to recognize these typical patterns of signals.

A self-learning network requires a learning set consisting of data provided for input. No output data are provided because, in this technique, we need to clarify the expectations from the network regarding the analysis of specific data. For example, if we apply the data in Figure 3.1 to learning without a teacher, we would use only the columns described as input data, rather than giving the network information from the column indicated by the red pointer .

A self-learning network would not be able to predict the levels of pollution in different cities, because it can't gain knowledge on its own. But by analyzing the data on different cities, the network may favor (without any help) a group of large industrial cities and learn to differentiate them from small country towns that lie in the center of agricultural regions.

The network will develop this distinction from the given input data by following the rule indicating that industrial cities are similar, and agricultural towns also share many common properties with each other.

Neural networks may (without any help) use a rule to distinguish those cities with good and bad weather and determine other classifications, depending only on values of observed input data. Notice that the self-learning network is very interesting from when comparing such network activities the activities of human brains.

People also have the ability to spontaneously classify the objects and phenomena they encounter. After a suitable classification has been executed, people and networks recognize another object as having characteristics belonging to a previously recognized class. Self-learning is very interesting, depending on the usage.

It requires knowledge that may be inaccessible or hard to gather. A neural network will collect all needed information and news segments without outside help. Now, you can imagine (for fun and for stimulating your imagination, rather than from real need) that a self-learning network with a television camera is sent in an unmanned space probe to Mars.

We don't know the conditions on Mars . We don't know which objects our probe should recognize or how many classes of objects will be found! But even without that information, the probe will land, and the network will begin the process of self-learning.

At first, it recognizes nothing and only observes its surroundings. However, over time, the process of spontaneous self-organization will allow the network to learn how to detect and differentiate various types of input signals: rocks from stones and plant forms from other living organisms.

If we give the network sufficient time, it will learn how to differentiate Martian men from Martian women, even though its creator did not know that Martian people existed! Of course, this self-learning probe on Mars vehicle is a hypothetical creation even though networks that create and recognize various patterns exist and are in common use. We might be interested in determining how many forms of a little known disease can be found in reality. Is a condition one sickness unit or several? How do the components differ? How can they be cured?

It might be enough to build a self-learning neural network **to store** the information on registered patients and their properties over a long period.

This network will yield information on how many typical groups of symptoms and signs were detected and which criteria can be used to classify patients into different groups. Applications of neural networks to goals like these might even lead to a Nobel Prize! This method of self-learning, surely, has many problems, which we'll describe later.

But self-learning undeniably has many advantages. You might be surprised to learn that this tool isn't as popular as it should be, given its many applications.

Methods of Gathering Information

Let's look at the process of learning with a teacher. How does a network gain and gather knowledge? Keep in mind, every neuron has many inputs, by which it receives the signals from other neurons and from network data to add to its processing results. The parameters, called weights, are combined with entry data. Each input signal is first modified by the weight ,and only later added to the other signals. If we change the values of the weights, a neuron will begin to function within the network in a new way, and ultimately the entire network will work in a different way. A network's learning capacities depends on the choice of weights, so that all neurons will perform the exact tasks demanded by the network A network may contain thousands of neurons, and every one of them may handle hundreds of inputs, so it's is impossible for all these inputs to create the necessary weights simultaneously and without direction.

We can, however, design and achieve learning by starting network activities with a certain random set of weights and gradually improving them. In every step of the learning process, the values of weights from one or several neurons undergo changes. The rules for change are set in such a way that every individual neuron can qualify which of its own weights must change, how (by being increased or decreased), and how much.

The teacher passes on the information about the necessary changes in the weights that can be used by the neuron.

Obviously, what doesn't change is the fact that the method of changing the weights runs through every neuron of the network, spontaneously and independently. In fact, it can occur without direct intervention by the person supervising this process.

What's more, the process of learning of one neuron is independent from how another neuron learns. Thus, learning can occur simultaneously in all neurons of a network (of course, this can only occur in a suitable network with an adequate electronic system, and not via a simulation program). This characteristic allows us to achieve very high speeds of learning and a surprisingly dynamic increase of skills of a network, which literally grows more and more intelligent before our eyes! We must stress a key point once again : a teacher need not get into the details of the process of learning. It's enough for the teacher to give a network an example of a correct solution. The network will compare its own solution, obtained from the example from the learning set, with the solution that was recorded as a model (most probably correct) in the learning set .

Algorithms of learning are constructed so that the knowledge about the value of an error is sufficient to allow a network to correct the values of its weights. Every neuron corrects its own weights on all entries, separately under the control of the specific algorithm, after it receives an error message.

It depicts a simple but efficient mechanism. Its systematic use causes the network to perfect its own activities, until it's finally able to solve all assignments from the learning set, on the grounds of generalization of this knowledge. It can also handle assignments that it will be introduced to at the examination stage. The manner of network learning described earlier is used most often, but some assignments (e.g., image recognition) don't require a network to have the exact value of a desired output signal.

For efficient learning, it's sufficient to give network only general information on a subject, whether its current behavior is correct, or not. At times, network experts speak about "rewards" and "punishments" in relation to the way all neurons in a network find and introduce proper corrections to their own activities without outside direction. This analogy to the training of animals isn't accidental.

Organizing Your Network

The variety of values of the weight coefficients in every neuron is counted based on specific rules (paradigms of networks). The numbers and varieties of the rules that are used today are extreme because most researchers try to position their own contributions to the domain of neural networks as new rules of learning.

We can now consider two basic rules of learning without using mathematics: the rule of the quickest fall, which is the basis of most algorithmic learning with a teacher, and the Hebb rule, which is simplest example of learning without a teacher.

The rule of the quickest fall relies on the receipt, by each of the neurons, of signals from the network or from other neurons. The signals give you the result from the first levels of processing the data. Neurons generate the output signal using their knowledge of the earlier settled values of all amplification factors (weights) of all entries and (maybe) the threshold. In the last section, we discussed many methods of marking the values of output signals by neurons based on input signal.

At every step of the method of learning, the value of the output signal of a neuron is compared to the teacher's answer within the learning process.

In that period of divergence, which occurs usually at the first step of the learning method, the neuron tries to find the difference between its own output signal and the value of the signal that the teacher indicates is correct. The neuron can then decide how to change the values of the weights to reduce the error.

It will be useful to understand the area of an error. You already know that the activity of a network relies on the values of the weight coefficients of the constituent neurons. If you know the set of all weight coefficients occurring in all neurons of the neural network, we will know how a network can act.

In particular, we can hypothesize a network of assignments, examples and solutions that are accessible as a part of a learning set. Each time the network provides its own answer to a question, you can compare its answer to the correct answer found in the learning set, thus revealing the network's errors.

Measuring the errors is always the difference between r the neural network's answer and the value of the result in m the learning set. To estimate the overall activities of networks with defining sets of weight coefficients in the neurons, you usually use the total of the squares of errors collected by the network for each case from the learning set. The errors are squared before addition to avoid the problem of mutual compensation of positive and negative errors. This results in heavy penalties for large errors.

Thus, a twice larger error will yield a quadruple component in the total result. Each state of good and bad learning of this neural network can be joined at the point on the horizontal (the light blue) surface shown in the figure, with its weight coefficient coordinates.

Just think about it: now you've localized those weight values in the neural network that comply with the location of the red point in the figure.

Examining a neural network by **meaning** all elements of the learning set will solve the total value of the errors. At the red point, you can place a red arrow pointing upwards.

The height will represent the final value of the error based on the vertical axis. To do the same steps using the blue pointer, just think about doing the same acts for all combinations of coefficients — that is, for the all points of the blue light.

We will see that many errors can be larger, and others, smaller. If you had the patience to examine your network many times, you will see the errors' surface placed over the different weights.

You can see many of them on the surface. This is the network giving several errors, and can be avoided. A neural network giving small errors is also possible.

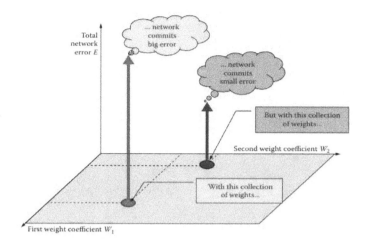

Usage of Momentum

One method of maximizing the learning speed without affecting stability is by using an additional component called momentum in the algorithm of learning. Momentum makes the process of learning broader by changing the weights on which the process depends and the current errors, and allows learning at the first step.

It allows for a comparison of learning with and without momentum and the process of changing the weight coefficients. We can show only two of them, and thus the drawing should be interpreted as a projection on the plane determined by the weight coefficient, wi, and the weight adaptation process, *wj*, that takes place in the *n* dimensional space of the weights.

We can see the behavior of only two inputs for a specific neuron of the network, but the processes in other neurons are similar.

The red (dark tone) points represent starting points (the setting before the start of learning the values of weight coefficients). The yellow points indicate the values of weight coefficients obtained during the learning steps. An assumption has been made that the minimum of the error function is attained at the point indicated by the plus sign (+).

The blue ellipse shows the outline of the stable error (the set of values of weight coefficients for which the process of learning maintains the same level of error). As shown in the figure, introducing momentum stabilizes the learning process as the weight coefficients don't change as violently or as frequently.

This will make the method more adequate as the consecutive points the way to the positive point faster. We use momentum for learning from a rule because it will improve the ratio of correct solutions obtained, and the execution costs are lower.

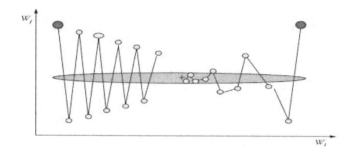

Questions

1. Briefly define the usage of momentum.

2. How can the network gather information?

3. List the factors that affect the organization of the network.

Chapter 4

Using Neural Networks

Using Neural Networks in a Practical Way

This will lead you to a site that accurately describes, step by step, all the required tasks for using these programs legally and at no cost. You'll need these programs to verify the information about neural networks in this book. Installing these programs on your computer will allow you to discover various features of neural networks, conduct interesting experiments, and even have fun with them.

Don't worry. Minimal experience of installing programs is required. Detailed installation instructions appear on the website. Note that updates of the software will quickly make the details in this book outdated. Despite that possibility, we should explain some of the procedures.

Downloading the programs from the site is very easy, and can be done with one click of the mouse.

However, obtaining the programs isn't enough. They're written in C# language and need to be installed libraries in .NET Framework (V. 2.0). All the required installation software is on the site.

The first step is installing the libraries. You might have some of these libraries installed on your computer already, so you might find this step unnecessary. If you're about this, you can skip the .NET Framework step, but we suggest you do it just in case.

If the right programs have already been installed on your computer, the install component will determine that it doesn't need to install anything . However, the site may contain newer versions of the libraries, in which case the installer will go to work. It's always wise to replace old software with newer versions. The new software will serve many purposes beyond those described in this book.

After you install the necessary .NET Framework libraries, on which further actions depend according to site guidelines, the installer will run again. This will allow you to install all sample programs automatically and painlessly.

You'll need them for performing the experiments covered in this book. When the installation is finished, you'll be able to access the programs via the start menu used for most programs. Performing .NET experiments will help you understand neural networks theoretically, as well as demonstrate their use for practical purposes.

If you don't believe this stop is simple, this is the difficult part of installation: the installer asks the user (1) where to install the programs and (2) who should have access.

The best response is to keep the default values and click on "Next". More inquisitive users have two more options: (1) downloading the source code and (2) installing the integrated development environment called Visual Studio.NET.

The first option allows you to download text versions of all the sample programs whose executable versions you'll use while studying with this book. It's very interesting to see how these programs have been designed and why they work as they do. Having the source code will allow you—if you dare—to modify the programs and perform even more interesting experiments. We must emphasize that the source codes aren't necessary if you simply want to use the programs. Obviously, having the codes will enable you to learn more and use the available resources in interesting ways. Obtaining the codes isn't a lot of work.

The second option, installing Visual Studio.NET, is for ambitious readers who want to modify our programs, design their own experiments, or write their own programs. We encourage readers to install Visual Studio.NET even if they only want to view the source code. Making viewing the code easier will only take a few extra minutes. Visual Studio.NET is very easy to install and use.

After installation, you'll be able to perform many more tasks, such as adding extern sets, diagnosing applications easily, and quickly generating complicated versions of the software.

Remember that installing the source codes and Visual Studio.NET are totally optional.

To run the sample programs that will allow you to create and test the neural network experiments described in this book, you need only install the .NET Framework (the first step) and sample programs (the second step).

What's next? To run any example, you must first choose the appropriate command from the Start/Programs/Neural Networks Examples menu. After making your selection, you may recreate and analyze every neural network described in this book with your computer. Initially your system will use a network whose shape and measurements were designed by us. After you gain access to the source code, you'll be able to modify and change whatever you want. The initial program will create networks live on your computer and allow you to teach, test, analyze, summarize, and examine them. This method of discovering the features of the neural networks—

by building and making them work—might even be far more fulfilling than learning the theory and attending lectures.

The way a network works depends on its structure and purpose. That is why we will discuss specific situations in subsequent chapters. We will start with image recognition, because it's the simplest network function to explain. This type of network receives an image as an input and, after categorization of the image based on previous learning, it produces an output.

This kind of network was discussed in the last chapter. A network handles the task of classifying geometric images by identifying printed and handwritten letters, planes, silhouettes, or human faces.

How does this type of network operate? To answer that, we must start from an absolutely simplified network that contains only one neuron. "What? You believe that a single neuron can't form a network, because a network should contain many neurons all connected to each other? The number of neurons doesn't truly matter, and so even a small network can produce interesting outputs.

The Capacity of a Single Neuron

As noted earlier, a neuron receives input signals and multiplies them by factors (weights assigned individually during the learning process), which are then added together and combined into a single output signal. To recap, you already know that summed signals in more complicated networks combine e to yield an output signal with an appropriate function (generally nonlinear). The behavior of our simplified linear neuron involves far less activity.

The value of the output signal depends on the level of acceptance between the signals of every input and the values of their weights. This rule applies ideally only to normalized input signals and weights. Without specific normalization, the value of an output signal may be treated as the measurement of similarity between assembly of the input signals and the assembly of their corresponding weights.

You might say that a neuron has its own memory and stores representations of its knowledge (patterns of input data as values of the weights) there. If the input signals match the recalled pattern, a neuron recognizes them as familiar and answers them with a strong output signal.

If the network finds no connection between the input signals and the pattern, the output signal is near 0 (no recognition). It's possible for a total contradiction to occur between the input signals and the weight values. A linear neuron generates a negative output signal in that case. The greater the contradiction between the neuron's image of the output signal and its real value, the stronger its negative output.

We encourage you to install and run a simple program named Example 01a to perform a few experiments. You'll learn even more about networks if you try to improve the program.

After initializing Example 01a, you'll see a window in the program. The text in the top section explains what we're going to do.

The blinking cursor signals that the program concerning flower characteristics is waiting for the weight of the neuron's input (in this case, the fragrant value). You can enter the value by typing a number, clicking the arrows next to the field, or using the up and down arrows on the keyboard.

After inserting the value for the fragrant feature, move on to the next field that corresponds to the second feature L color.

Let's assume that you want your neuron to prefer colorful and fragrant flowers, with more weight for color. After receiving an appropriate answer, the window of the program will look like this program, and every other one you'll use allows you to change your decision and choose another input. The program will try to update the results of its calculations.

After we input the feature data (which ,in fact, are weight values), we can study how the neuron works. You can input various sets of data, as shown in Figure 4.4, and the program will compute the resulting output signal and its meaning. Remember that you can change the neuron's preferences and the flower description at any time.

If you're using a mouse or arrow keys to input data, you don't have to click the "recalculate" button every time you want to see the result; calculations are executed automatically. When you input a number from the keyboard, you have to click the button because the computer doesn't know if you finished entering the number or left to go get a tuna sandwich.

The next stage is to experiment with a neuron in an unusual situation. The point of the experiment in this window is to observe how the neuron reacts to an object that differs from its ideal colorful and fragrant flower. We showed the neuron a flower full of colors with no fragrance. As you can see, the neuron liked this flower too!

You'll find "playing" with the Example 01a program to be a worthwhile exercise. As you input various data sets, you'll quickly see how a neuron functions according to a simple rule. The neuron treats its weight as a model for the input signal it wants to recognize. When it receives a combination of signals that corresponds to the weight, the neuron "finds" something familiar and reacts enthusiastically by generating a strong output signal. A neuron can signal indifference by a low output signal, and even indicate aversion via a negative output, because its nature is to react positively to a signal it recognizes.

Careful examination will show that the behavior of a neuron depends only on the angle between the vector of the weight and the vector of the input signal. We will use Example 01b to further demonstrate a neuron's likes and dislikes by presenting an ideal flower as a point (or vector) in the input space.

When you set the preferences of a neuron, you tell it, for example, to prefer fragrant and colorful flowers. Fragrance and color are separate weight vectors. You can draw two axes. On the horizontal axis, you can note the values of the first feature (fragrance), and indicate the values of the second

feature (color) on the vertical axis. You can mark the neuron's preferences on the axes. The point where these coordinates meet indicates the neuron's preferences.

A neuron that values only the fragrance of a flower and is indifferent to the color will be represented by a point located maximally to the right (a high value for the first coordinate), but on the horizontal axis, will be set at a low number or zero. A puttyroot flower has beautiful colors and a weak an sometimes unpleasant smell. The puttyroot would be located high on the vertical axis (high color value) and t left on the horizontal axis to indicate a weak or unpleasant smell. Flower color is valued on the vertical axis and fragrance, on the horizontal axis. You can treat any object that you'd like a neuron to mark with this technique.

Questions

1. Using the .Net framework, implement a neural
   network.

www.ingramcontent.com/pod-product-compliance
Lightning Source LLC
Chambersburg PA
CBHW070854070326
40690CB00009B/1831

* 9 7 8 1 7 1 8 8 9 8 4 2 4 *